MW00615148

$\mathcal{A}$ daughter is someone you laugh with,
dream with, and love with all your heart.

 Author Unknown

Blue Mountain Arts®

"The Language of the Heart…" series

For an Amazing Son

Marriage Is a Promise to Love

Mothers & Daughters

A Sister Is Forever

To a Beautiful Daughter

True Friendship Is a Gift

The Language of the Heart...

To a
Beautiful
Daughter

A Blue Mountain Arts® Collection

Edited by Patricia Wayant

Blue Mountain Press™

Boulder, Colorado

Copyright © 2019 by Blue Mountain Arts, Inc.

All rights reserved. No part of this publication may be reproduced, stored in a retrieval system or transmitted in any form or by any means, electronic, mechanical, photocopying, recording or otherwise, without the written permission of the publisher.

We wish to thank Susan Polis Schutz for permission to reprint the following poems that appear in this publication: "I looked at you today…," "…a star glimmering in the sky…," "Know yourself…," "You were brought…," and "You are a shining…." Copyright © 1984, 1986, 1991 by Stephen Schutz and Susan Polis Schutz. All rights reserved.

Library of Congress Control Number: 2019900054
ISBN: 978-1-68088-291-9

◼ and Blue Mountain Press are registered in U.S. Patent and Trademark Office. Certain trademarks are used under license.

Acknowledgments appear on the last page.

Handmade paper used on cover made in Thailand.
Printed and assembled in China.
First Printing: 2019

♻ Interior of this book is printed on recycled paper.

Blue Mountain Arts, Inc.
P.O. Box 4549, Boulder, Colorado 80306

Contents

(Authors listed in order of first appearance)

Ashley Rice
Cheryl Barker
Lorrie Westfall
Susan Polis Schutz
Darlene Helms Griffin
W. Bruce Cameron
Dwayne Johnson
Frances M. Frost
Alan Beck
Jacqueline Schiff
Shirley Chowdhary
Mary Adisano
Douglas Pagels
Stephen J. Lyons
Eric Roth
Ralph Waldo Emerson
James T. Slater
Amy L. Kuo
Lois Carruthers
Vicky Lafleur

Ashli Mazer
Barbara Cage
Brenda A. Morris
Natasha Josefowitz
Deanna Beisser
Linda Sackett-Morrison
Heather Swain
Jean Lamey
Eleanor Roosevelt
Albert Einstein
Julie Anne Ford
Jenny Studenroth
Jane Almarie Lewis
Ani DiFranco
Sheryl Sandberg
Rebecca Barlow Jordan
Kellie L. McCracken
Linda Pastan
T. L. Nash
Vickie M. Worsham

Beautiful Daughter

You are so important to me.
Ever since you came into this world,
I can't imagine my life without you in it.
You are rare and unique and special
and always thinking of other people.

I've loved watching you grow,
and I am so proud of who you've become.
I want you to know that whatever you do,
you can always count on me to be there for you.
I hope you always follow your dreams
and stand by your beliefs as you do now.

You are so strong and beautiful,
and you will make
a great contribution to the world.
I love you for
everything you are.

 Ashley Rice

You Are a Blessing
to All Who Know You

*D*o you know that you inspire me
with your zest for living life?

You're never afraid
to try new things,
you're always ready
for a new adventure,
and along the way,
you spread sunshine,
touching others with your kindness.

Yes, sweet daughter,
you inspire me
to live life to the fullest.

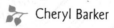 Cheryl Barker

*A*ll throughout my life, I have realized over and over: I've never been more blessed than when I was given the gift of being your parent.

All throughout your life, you have amazed me and impressed me and given me thousands of reasons to love you more than I already do.

Over the course of time, there have been so many changes in our days and in everything around us. But one thing always stays the same…

My feeling that you are more than just the brightest star in my sky…
>   you're one of the
>   most special people
>   in the whole wide world.

 Lorrie Westfall

I Love You Every Minute of Every Day

I looked at you today
and saw the same beautiful eyes
that looked at me with love
when you were a baby
I looked at you today
and saw the same beautiful mouth
that made me cry when you
    first smiled at me
when you were a baby
It was not long ago
that I held you in my arms
long after you fell asleep
and I just kept rocking you
all night long
I looked at you today
and saw my beautiful daughter
no longer a baby
but a beautiful person
with a full range of emotions
feelings, ideas and goals

Every day is exciting
as I continue to watch you grow
I want you to always know that
in good and in bad times
I will love you
and that no matter what you do
or how you think
or what you say
you can depend on
my support, guidance
friendship and love
every minute of every day

 Susan Polis Schutz

Daughter, my memories of you
    always take me back through the years...
memories of an infant
    so sweet and small and trusting,
memories of a toddler
    giggling with the joy of childhood,
memories of a young girl smiling
    and playing with her friends,
memories of your teen years
    full of change and doubt and growth.

And now, I see a lovely, gentle woman —
    my best friend, the baby I held,
        the daughter with whom I shared
        secret jokes, special talks,
    laughter and victories, tears and defeats,
and gentle guidance into a world of hope.

I feared that I might have spoiled
    you many years ago,
but you spoiled me instead...
with boundless joy and soaring pride
    and a love that grew as you did.

 Darlene Helms Griffin

$\mathcal{T}$otally unbidden, an image of my daughter slips into my head, not as she appeared in the sonogram, when she looked to me like a potato in a microwave, but just yesterday, when I happened to stop by her office and saw her in a conference room, running a meeting with her staff. She looked like a grownup.

My little girl is all grown up.

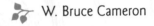 W. Bruce Cameron

$\mathcal{W}$hen I held her when she was born,
I held her in these two hands and I said
to her, "I will always, always take care of
you. For the rest of your life, you are safe."

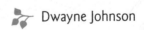 Dwayne Johnson

Of a Small Daughter Walking Outdoors

Easy, wind!
Go softly here!
She is small
And very dear.

She is young
And cannot say
Words to chase
The wind away.

She is new
To walking, so
Wind, be kind
And gently blow

On her ruffled head,
On grass and clover.
Easy, wind…
She'll tumble over!

 Frances M. Frost

Sweet Daughter of Mine…

Did you know
that my world changed forever
when you came into my life?
No one could have prepared me
for the depth of love
that sprang into my heart for you
from the very moment you were born.
You truly are a treasure,
and I will cherish you all my life.
I will brag about you and show you off
every time I get the chance.
And though I don't know how it's possible,
you become more dear to me
with every year that passes by.

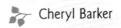 Cheryl Barker

What Is a Girl?

Little girls are the nicest things that happen to people. They are born with a little bit of angel-shine about them, and though it wears thin sometimes, there is always enough left to lasso your heart — even when they are sitting in the mud, or crying temperamental tears, or parading up the street in Mother's best clothes.

A little girl can be sweeter (and badder) oftener than anyone else in the world. She can jitter around, and stomp, and make funny noises that frazzle your nerves, yet just when you open your mouth, she stands there demure with that special look in her eyes. A girl is Innocence playing in the mud, Beauty standing on its head, and Motherhood dragging a doll by the foot....

God borrows from many creatures to make a little girl. He uses the song of a bird, the squeal of a pig, the stubbornness of a mule, the antics of a monkey, the spryness of a grasshopper, the curiosity of a cat, the speed of a gazelle, the slyness of a fox, the softness of a kitten, and to top it all off He adds the mysterious mind of a woman.

Who else can cause you more grief, joy, irritation, satisfaction, embarrassment, and genuine delight than this combination of Eve, Salome, and Florence Nightingale? She can muss up your home, your hair, and your dignity — spend your money, your time, and your patience — and just when your temper is ready to crack, her sunshine peeks through and you've lost again.

Yes, she is a nerve-racking nuisance, just a noisy bundle of mischief. But when your dreams tumble down and the world is a mess — when it seems you are pretty much of a fool after all — she can make you a king when she climbs on your knee and whispers, "I love you best of all!"

— Alan Beck

I'm Fortunate to Have a Daughter like You

To have a daughter like you is to feel proud when I wake up each day. In spite of the mistakes I made in raising you, you never let them shape your future. You walked the path to success and triumphed with your positive attitude, your talents, and the lessons you learned.

To have a daughter like you is to feel peace in my heart. I don't have to hover over you, worry needlessly about you, or wonder if you're safe and secure. In the depths of my soul, I know you are a strong, capable, accomplished woman who is exactly where she wants to be in her life.

To have a daughter like you is to hear the music of joy and laughter wherever I go. Your can-do attitude, boundless energy, and enthusiasm for making the best of every situation are contagious and fun. Your spirited nature uplifts and inspires me.

To have a daughter like you is to be in the company of a best friend who holds my hand, gives me hugs, and walks with me through my troubles. In you, I have a companion who shares with me a special understanding of why we are blessed to be friends. To have a daughter like you is to walk with pride for all you are and with happiness in my heart for all we share.

Jacqueline Schiff

You Are Beautiful in Every Way

You are beautiful. Embrace it. Know it. Own it. I know that you don't believe me. I know that when you look in the mirror you focus on the hair that is out of place, the pimple on your face, the abs that aren't defined, the thighs that you don't like… There are always going to be people in the world to point out those things. So what? The measure of a good person is not the size of their thighs…. It's the kindness that you show to your little brother when he is looking for attention, it's your integrity and your immense and overwhelming sense of goodness.

— Shirley Chowdhary

*I*n my eyes, daughter, you are someone who has been blessed with not only outer beauty but inner beauty. This is the kind of beauty that is everlasting. Time can never take that away from you.

 Mary Adisano

*Y*ou're not just a beautiful daughter. You're an exquisite, rare, and extraordinary person. All the different facets of your life — the ones you reveal to the rest of the world and the ones known only to those you're close to — are so amazing. And as people look even deeper, I know they can't help but see how wonderful you are inside.

 Douglas Pagels

Fatherly Advice

The final list of fatherly advice: clip coupons and always buy generic. Memorize some lines of poetry. Learn to play a musical instrument. Exercise, but never weigh yourself. Make a lot of money and then give it all away. Learn the names of flowers, plants, and birds. Sleep with the windows open. Recycle. Eat out only in small-town cafes where the waitress is also the cook, bartender, and daycare coordinator. Volunteer in the community. Cultivate solitude. Forgive yourself. Bring your own bag to the grocery store.... Don't run the water needlessly when brushing your teeth. Use less of everything. Hug a tree. Don't spit. Be of good cheer.

— Stephen J. Lyons

Don't stress out about things you have no control over. Sometimes what is... just is. And don't be afraid to ask for advice. There are people who love you and care about you and would love to help you in any way they can.

— Douglas Pagels

*F*or what it's worth: It's never too late or, in my case, too early to be whoever you want to be. There's no time limit. Start whenever you want. You can change or stay the same. There are no rules to this thing. We can make the best or the worst of it. I hope you make the best of it. And I hope you see things that startle you. I hope you feel things you never felt before. I hope you meet people with a different point of view. I hope you live a life you're proud of. If you find that you're not, I hope you have the strength to start all over again.

 Eric Roth

*F*inish every day and be done with it.... You have done what you could; some blunders and absurdities no doubt crept in; forget them as soon as you can. Tomorrow is a new day; you shall begin it well and serenely, and with too high a spirit to be cumbered with your old nonsense. This day is all that is good and fair. It is too dear, with its hopes and invitations, to waste a moment on rotten yesterdays.

Ralph Waldo Emerson

In My Daughter's Eyes

In my daughter's eyes I am a hero
I am strong and wise and I know no fear
But the truth is plain to see
She was sent to rescue me
I see who I want to be
In my daughter's eyes

In my daughter's eyes everyone is equal
Darkness turns to light and the
World is at peace
This miracle God gave to me
Gives me strength when I am weak
I find reason to believe
In my daughter's eyes

And when she wraps her hand
Around my finger
Oh it puts a smile in my heart
Everything becomes a little clearer
I realize what life is all about
It's hanging on when your heart
Has had enough
It's giving more when you feel like giving up
I've seen the light
It's in my daughter's eyes

In my daughter's eyes I can see the future
A reflection of who I am and what will be
Though she'll grow and someday leave
Maybe raise a family
When I'm gone I hope you see how happy
She made me
For I'll be there
In my daughter's eyes

James T. Slater

A Mother's Joy

When I look at you, I see years of memories and decades of potential. You have already changed my world in spectacular ways, and now I see you impact the rest of the world in wonderful ways as well. I am honored to be your mother.

 Amy L. Kuo

You are the sparkle in my eyes and the pride in my heart. You are the courage that gives me strength and the love that gives me life. You are my inspiration and the best gift I ever received. You are my child, and I feel so blessed that I am allowed to be a part of your life.

Lois Carruthers

*T*hrough the years, Daughter, I watched you grow, change, and constantly question everything. When you were little, there was an overwhelming feeling inside me that wanted to hold you close and keep you safe and warm all your life. Yet as the years passed, I realized that I couldn't do that. You have always been a child full of wonder, and to keep you so close to me would have deprived you of experiencing life's wonders.

Now, after years of letting you go your own way and watching you become a beautiful young lady, our roles have changed. You are still my daughter, and I am still your parent, but most precious of all is the fact that we have become good friends, and we have a friendship that will stand the test of time.

I'll always cherish the wonder and joy of watching you grow into a beautiful young lady. I'll always be proud to say, "This is my daughter." But most of all, I'm proud to say that you are my best friend.

 Vicky Lafleur

I wish for my daughter…

The ability to know her self-worth and to never allow another being to ever make her feel incapable. That she realizes her value in this life is irreplaceable.

The confidence to walk away. In relationships, in work, and in life, I hope she understands we are granted one life to live and if her instinct is calling her to move on, that she should trust it and start again.

To always lead with kindness. That acceptance and love are not signs of weakness but strength. That living a life with open arms is the ultimate in living authentically….

The strength to know she is capable of all things great and all things good. Her mind, her heart, her hands are powerful, and she alone can move her own mountains or use her own abilities to make something good for someone else.

To strive for contentment versus happiness. That happiness is how she feels in a moment and to understand that it is temporary. Contentment is a mindset and lifestyle when her whole soul will feel alive and good.

To find and hold on to her passions. To realize that she is meant to dream and to dream big and to never give up on the things that spark her soul and the things she can't fall asleep to because they stir excitement....

To possess the will to always stand up and fight for herself, her beliefs, and for her dreams. To realize that at the end of the day, she will only stare back at herself when she looks in the mirror. So, she should be the person she wants to see.

Ashli Mazer

A Daughter Is...

...one of the greatest blessings one could ever have. Her smile is a precious sight that you treasure each time you see it, and the sound of her laughter always brings joy to your heart.

 Barbara Cage

...a little piece of yourself looking back at you.

Brenda A. Morris

...the only person
I can comfortably shop with
and not feel impatient
when she tries on things forever
or worry that I'm taking too long
in deciding between two dresses.

Natasha Josefowitz

...God's way of saying, "Thought you could use a lifelong friend."

Author Unknown

...a miracle that never
　　ceases to be miraculous...
full of beauty
　　and forever beautiful...
loving and caring
　　and truly amazing.

 Deanna Beisser

...the essence of joy and the true meaning of life.
She's the part of you that you're most proud of, a
rare and treasured gift.

　　　　　　　　　Linda Sackett-Morrison

...a star glimmering in the sky
a wonder, a sweetness
a perception, a delight...
everything beautiful
A daughter is
love

　　　　Susan Polis Schutz

What Every Parent Wants for Their Daughter

I want my daughter to be bold in life. To take risks and go out on limbs. I want her to never be afraid to try something potentially rewarding because it may disrupt the status quo of her life. To do that, she's going to need to be self-sufficient, ingenious, and have healthy relationships — with people, with food, and with money. While she's young, I want my daughter to learn to question her desires, to learn the difference between wants and needs, and to be comfortable opting out of socially mandated "must haves" and expensive fads.... But I also want her to know when it's okay to cut the purse strings and let loose a little.

 Heather Swain

$\mathcal{D}$aughter, I want you to be proud of yourself for being a good person. What matters isn't the awards you receive, but the way you treat other people.

I want you to be proud of your heritage. Choose to live your life in ways that honor your ancestors. Those who paved the way for you have passed on the torch to you. Carry it with dignity and responsibility.

I want you to always be a woman of action. Dreams are important, but only acting on them will make them happen.

I want you to know the strength and abundance of my love. Close your eyes for a moment and feel my love wrapped around you. Feel it surrounding you wherever you go.

I want you to always know I'm thinking of you with love, pride, and the highest admiration for the beautiful woman you've become.

— Jacqueline Schiff

You Will Always Have
a Family Who Loves You

We are family. We have love and loyalty and faith in each other. We have memories that light our minds like sunshine and others that bring strength through our family ties. We have family customs and traditions that bring us together across the miles and give us our legacy. We share a history of family reunions, family albums, and old scrapbooks of memorabilia that only we can appreciate. We have different generations who all pitch in through thick and thin and welcome everyone's contributions.

We've shared hugs and heartaches, laughter and struggles, hard work and passionate play. Through it all, our bond keeps us from falling too far or being unanchored in the spaces of the world. We have hopes and dreams more easily shared with each other than with most other people. We have prayers of protection for one another and also opinions we feel free to agree or disagree with. We are family — with different voices, life choices, and styles. But above all we are one — because we are family.

 Jacqueline Schiff

Always Believe
in Yourself, Daughter

*K*now yourself —
what you can do
and want to do in life
Set goals
and work hard to achieve them
Have fun every day in every way
Be creative —
it is an expression of your feelings
Be sensitive in viewing the world
Believe in the family
as a stable and rewarding way of life
Believe in love
as the most complete
and important emotion possible
Believe that you are
an important part of
everyone's life that you touch
Believe in yourself
and know that you are loved

 Susan Polis Schutz

Within you is an ideal,
a voice of youth,
and a promise of achievement
still to come.
Within your hands
are special gifts and talents.
Within your mind is the
source of your dreams.
Within you is the strength
to carry your dreams to completion.
Within your heart is the desire
to meet the world on your own terms,
and I never doubt that you will.
Within you rest my hopes and dreams.
You are strong; you are wise;
you have a dream.
You have a spirit and confidence
    I never knew; you have faith.
You are your own person,
    and you always will be.
Within you, Daughter,
is something so precious and rare.
Within you is the promise of the future,
and I believe in you.

— Jean Lamey

Don't Ever Lose Your Curiosity...

I think, at a child's birth, if a mother could ask a fairy godmother to endow it with the most useful gift, that gift would be curiosity.

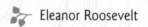 Eleanor Roosevelt

*T*he important thing is not to stop questioning. Curiosity has its own reason for existence. One cannot help but be in awe when he contemplates the mysteries of eternity, of life, of the marvelous structure of reality. It is enough if one tries merely to comprehend a little of this mystery each day.

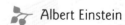 Albert Einstein

$\mathcal{L}$et nothing hold you back from exploring
your wildest fantasies, wishes, and
aspirations.
Don't be afraid to follow your dreams
wherever they lead you.
Open your eyes to their beauty;
open your mind to their magic;
open your heart to their possibilities.
Only by dreaming will you ever discover
who you are, what you want,
and what you can do.
Don't be afraid to take risks,
to become involved,
to make a commitment.
Do whatever it takes to make
your dreams come true.

 Julie Anne Ford

Trust in Yourself

When the world gets complicated and the answers are unclear, you don't need to waste too much time canvassing others for their opinions. Do your own research, be your own guide, and listen to what your intuition tells you. You will not always be right, honey, I promise you this. You will make mistakes, so many mistakes that sometimes you'll wonder if you're capable of getting it right. But that's the important part. In the mistakes you find your pathway to the resolution. Embrace them, forgive yourself, and move on....

And most importantly, love yourself, honey. Love yourself like I love you. Cherish your precious heart, strong mind, and beautiful body. Keep a photograph of yourself in your wallet like I learned to do, so when you are out in the world making choices you can open it up and glance at that face to remember who you need to take care of. Be who you are on the inside, all the time. And don't forget that it's okay to change. Don't forget that you deserve all the love in the world, and make sure that you get it.

 Jenny Studenroth

*D*uring troubled times —
or even during happy, carefree times —
remember the depth and core of who you are.
Remember your strength and inner light.
Remember where you came from
and where you've been.
Remember that nothing can destroy you.
Life can only make you bigger, better,
    and brighter…
if you allow it to do so.

 Jane Almarie Lewis

*A*gainst all odds, against all examples
that you see around you, trust yourself….
To emerge into yourself, to find your
own voice, you have to trust in it, even
if nobody around you is. There's such a
power in that.

 Ani DiFranco

What It Means to Be a Success

I do not believe that there is one definition of success or happiness. Not all women want careers. Not all women want children. Not all women want both. I would never advocate that we should all have the same objectives. Many people are not interested in acquiring power, not because they lack ambition, but because they are living their lives as they desire. Some of the most important contributions to our world are made by caring for one person at a time. We each have to chart our own unique course and define which goals fit our lives, values, and dreams.

 Sheryl Sandberg

$\mathcal{R}$emember…
it's not how much you accomplish in life
that really counts,
but how much you give to others.
It's not how high you build your dreams
that makes a difference,
but how high your faith can climb.
It's not how many goals you reach,
but how many lives you touch.
It's not who you know that matters,
but who you are inside.

 Rebecca Barlow Jordan

$\mathcal{A}$lways. Unconditionally.
Follow your own heart.
Understand that persistence, hard work,
    and determination are the keys to success.

 Barbara Cage

You Have Grown Up to Be Such a Beautiful Woman

You were brought
into this world
a beautiful little girl
born of love
who would one day
grow up to be
a beautiful woman
full of love
I tried to teach you
important values and morals
I tried to show you
how to be strong and honest
    gentle and sensitive
I tried to explain to you
why you need to set and achieve
    your own goals

I tried to show you
the importance of being independent
    and confident
I tried to express
the need to reach out to people
I tried to emphasize
the beauty of nature
I tried to demonstrate
the extreme importance of family
And I tried every day to set an example
that you could look up to
though I am sure that I failed
to do this on many occasions
But one thing that I have always done
and will continue to do forever
is to be very proud of you
and to appreciate, support
and love you
and to be here for you whenever
    you need me
my beautiful daughter

 Susan Polis Schutz

You may be grown now,
but occasionally I still see
the little girl in you.
It may be just the way
you turn your head
or a certain look in your eyes,
but in that instant I'm reminded
that this woman is still my little girl.

 Cheryl Barker

Of course, I always knew
that someday you would be
a woman building your own life,
chasing dreams you've spent
      years creating.
It came just a little too fast.

 Kellie L. McCracken

When I taught you
at eight to ride
a bicycle, loping along
beside you
as you wobbled away
on two round wheels,
my own mouth rounding
in surprise when you pulled
ahead down the curved
path of the park,
I kept waiting
for the thud
of your crash as I
sprinted to catch up,
while you grew
smaller, more breakable
with distance,
pumping, pumping
for your life, screaming
with laughter,
the hair flapping
behind you like a
handkerchief waving
goodbye.

Linda Pastan

I Couldn't Be More Proud of You

From holding you in my arms when you were little…
to holding you in my heart so lovingly every single day,
I have always felt like the luckiest parent of all.

You are the reason behind so many of the smiles in
my life, and I know, without a doubt, that you are the
sweetest gift imaginable. To me, you will always be the
most beautiful person on the face of this earth.

You make my heart absolutely overflow with all the
happiness and gratitude you inspire in my life. You
make me feel like every prayer I've ever whispered has
been answered… and every dream I've ever wanted
has come true.

And I have a great imagination, but I can't even begin
to imagine that anyone could be more proud of their
daughter… more than I am of you.

— Douglas Pagels

You are a shining
example of what a
daughter can be —
loving and compassionate
beautiful and good
honest and principled
determined and independent
sensitive and intelligent
You are a shining
example of what every
parent wishes their
daughter were
and I am so very
proud of
you

— Susan Polis Schutz

Ten Things I Want You to Always Remember

1. You are a miracle.

2. Never give up without first giving it your very best.

3. Don't let someone's opinion of you matter more than <u>your</u> opinion of yourself.

4. If it challenges you… do it. Even if you're afraid.

5. There's no such thing as failure if you learned something.

6. What you do in life has a ripple effect… make sure you like the waves you create.

7. If you can help someone, do it. Not because you have to, but because you want to.

8. Create healthy boundaries in every area of your life.

9. Always have faith, even when it's hard to see beyond your trials.

10. I love you with all my heart, Daughter, and I am always here for you.

T. L. Nash

I Hope Your Dreams
Come True

You are completely amazing! I hope you always find whatever you are looking for.

May you always fight the tough battles and go after all the sparkling stars that you have your heart set on capturing. I hope you set goals for yourself and achieve them, believing in all you can do and be.

May you chase after rainbows and always remember your childhood innocence.

I hope you always live with optimism and idealism as your guideposts and roadmaps to the future. You are so strong, independent, and brave, and I have had great pride watching you grow into the amazing woman that you've become.

May you reach your greatest aspirations, believe in miracles, and dream big.

You are a unique treasure to me and to so many other people. I hope with all my heart that your greatest dreams come true and that you find true happiness and more in your ever-changing days.

— Ashley Rice

Daughter,
You Are My Life's
Greatest Gift

*M*emories come flooding back to me
　　as I look back over the years.
I want to hold on to you and at the same time
　　watch you fly high and free.
You have such spirit
　　and a character all your own.
You are a doer and an achiever
　　of what you believe in.
I'm so proud of the dreams you have
　　and the conviction you have
to make those dreams come true.
Your world is bright, new,
　　and bursting with possibilities.

It's so easy to remember
    your very first steps
and how I held out my hand
    for you to hold.
As each year passes
    you take more steps,
and some of these will eventually
    lead you away from me —
but always remember that my hand
    and my heart are forever here
        for you.
You will always be my daughter,
    but I have also discovered in you
a rare and precious friend.
You have been life's greatest gift to me,
and I love you so much.

 Vickie M. Worsham

Acknowledgments

We gratefully acknowledge the permission granted by the following authors, publishers, and authors' representatives to reprint poems or excerpts in this publication: Trident Media Group LLC for "Totally unbidden, an image of…" from 8 SIMPLE RULES FOR MARRYING MY DAUGHTER by W. Bruce Cameron. Copyright © 2008 by W. Bruce Cameron. All rights reserved. Dwayne Johnson for "When I held her…" by Dwayne Johnson from *Oprah's Master Class "Dwayne Johnson,"* Episode 502 (Season 5), first aired November 15, 2015 on OWN. Copyright © 2015 by Dwayne Johnson. All rights reserved. Shirley Chowdhary for "You are beautiful…" from "A Letter to My Daughter — The World Is Your Oyster," *Huffpost – AU Edition* (blog), September 29, 2015, http://www.huffingtonpost.com.au/shirley-chowdhary/a-letter-to-my-daughter-t_b_8204872.html. Copyright © 2015 by Shirley Chowdhary. All rights reserved. Stephen J. Lyons for "Fatherly Advice" from LANDSCAPE OF THE HEART: WRITINGS ON DAUGHTERS AND JOURNEYS. Copyright © 2016 by Stephen J. Lyons. All rights reserved. Paramount Pictures Inc./Warner Bros. Entertainment Inc. for "For what it's worth…" from THE CURIOUS CASE OF BENJAMIN BUTTON screenplay by Eric Roth, based on the short story by F. Scott Fitzgerald. Copyright © 2006 by Paramount Pictures Inc./Warner Bros. Entertainment Inc. All rights reserved. Alfred Music, a division of Alfred Publishing LLC, for "In My Daughter's Eyes," words and music by James T. Slater. Copyright © 2003 by Reservoir Media Management, Inc. and Diversion Music (BMI). All rights administered by Reservoir Media Management, Inc. Reservoir Media Music (ASCAP) administered by Alfred Music. All rights reserved. Ashli Mazer for "I wish for my daughter…," *Backwards n High Heels* (blog), July 24, 2017, http://backwardsnhighheels.com/2017/07/24/i-wish-for-my-daughter. Copyright © 2017 by Ashli Mazer. All rights reserved. Natasha Josefowitz for "…the only person I can comfortably…" from NATASHA'S WORDS FOR FAMILIES. Copyright © 1986 by Natasha Josefowitz. All rights reserved. Heather Swain for "I want my daughter to be bold…" by Heather Swain from BECAUSE I LOVE HER: 34 WOMEN WRITERS REFLECT ON THE MOTHER-DAUGHTER BOND, edited by Andrea N. Richesin. Copyright © 2009 by Heather Swain. All rights reserved. *Momtastic* for "When the world gets complicated…" from "A Letter to My Daughter About Loving Herself" by Jenny Studenroth, *momtastic* (blog), http://www.momtastic.com/parenting/694495-a-letter-to-my-daughter. Copyright © 2019 by Jenny Studenroth. All rights reserved. Ani DiFranco for "Against all odds…" in "Connection, Community, and the Feminine Voice — Ani DiFranco," from an episode on *Emerging Women* (podcast), 2013, https://emergingwomen.com/podcast/ani-difranco-connection-community-and-the-feminine-voice/. Copyright © 2013 by Ani DiFranco. All rights reserved. Alfred A. Knopf, an imprint of the Knopf Doubleday Publishing Group, a division of Penguin Random House LLC, for "I do not believe that there…" from LEAN IN: WOMEN, WORK, AND THE WILL TO LEAD by Sheryl Sandberg with Nell Scovell. Copyright © 2013 by Lean In Foundation. All rights reserved. W. W. Norton & Company, Inc. and Jean V. Naggar Literary Agency, Inc. for "When I taught you…" from THE IMPERFECT PARADISE by Linda Pastan. Copyright © 1988 by Linda Pastan. All rights reserved. T. L. Nash for "Ten Things I Want You to Always Remember." Copyright © 2019 by T. L. Nash. All rights reserved.

A careful effort has been made to trace the ownership of selections used in this anthology in order to obtain permission to reprint copyrighted material and give proper credit to the copyright owners. If any error or omission has occurred, it is completely inadvertent, and we would like to make corrections in future editions provided that written notification is made to the publisher:

BLUE MOUNTAIN ARTS, INC., P.O. Box 4549, Boulder, Colorado 80306